Poetry To End Prohibition

Poetry To End Prohibition

Thundercloud Repairian

James Arthur Warren

Thundercloud Repairian

Thundercloud Repairian

CONTENTS

1	Forward	1
2	The Tawny Frogmouth On Prohibition	3
3	Love and Lust in Nimbin	8
4	Ode to the drumming circle in Nimbin	10
5	The Fire's Aftermath	11
6	This is the sign you are looking for: Gurrimah	12
7	This is the sign you are looking for and? Part 2 Shane the Cannabis Dealer	13
8	Just	16
9	An Oasis	18
10	Legalise Lettuce	19

CONTENTS

11 | The Yoga Wars — 21

12 | Burn the Parliament — 23

13 | Medical Cannabis Workshop — 27

14 | — 29

15 | The Notice Board of Dreams — 30

16 | Stoned or High? — 33

17 | They locked up my nana — 36

18 | Stinky Bong Bill — 38

19 | — 40

20 | Crack hole — 41

21 | Pizzaster — 44

22 | The voices of the dead — 46

23 | Healing Herb Haiku — 48

24 | Prohibition is corrosive — 49

25 | End Prohibition for my Grandma — 51

CONTENTS

26 | Weeds 52

27 | Shakespeare Inhaled 53

28 | Tawny Frogmouth's Pain- The Sixth Visit 54

29 | Dedicated to Daniel the Lion 56

30 | Daniel Walmsley 57

31 | After word 59

32 | The Seventh Visit of the Tawny Frogmouth 60

33 | The End of Prohibition 61

Forward

POETRY TO END PROHIBITION :
Written by Thundercloud Repairian aka James Arthur Warren
™& © Thundercloud Repairian All Rights Reserved
Published by THUNDERCLOUD REPAIRIAN in 144 Bradley Street Guyra NSW 2365
Email: 1english1@gmail.com
Copyright 2020
CONDITIONS OF SALE
This edition of this book is sold subject to the condition that it shall not by way of trade or otherwise be lent, copied, re-sold, hired out or otherwise circulated without the publisher's written consent, in any from, binding or cover other than that in which it is published and without a similar condition, including this condition being imposed on the subsequent publisher.

Thundercloud Repairian ™ @(c) THUNDERCLOUD REPAIRIAN

Thundercloud gratefully and respectfully acknowledges the Widjabal/Wyabal Bundjalung people as the traditional custodians of the land where this poetry was written

The first time I saw the Tawny frogmouth I took the photo on the cover. The next morning I found him dead on the ground, That was in 2016.

In 2019 Living at Lillian Rock, a healing place I saw the Tawny Frogmouth and his family again.

The Tawny Frogmouth on Prohibition poem was written over a period of months. The first visit from the Tawny Frogmouth came one morning before Nimbin Mardi Grass in 2019. He appeared twice more that weekend and each morning I wrote down the messages that he brought me.

I ended up with five large poems including one on women's incarceration. I took the five poems honed, edited and practiced until perfect and delivered them in the 2019 Nimbin Performance Poetry World Cup.

It was a while before I saw him again
the tawny frogmouth came and told me about his pain
The last time I saw him this is what he said,
"Publish your book I heard it in my head
Publish your book to eliminate my pain
Prohibition is driving me fucking insane"
Prohibition destroys lives of the rich and the poor
Please change this insanity, please I implore"
Love and infinity for eternity with Poetry to End Prohibition
James Arthur Warren
Aka Thundercloud Repairian

The Tawny Frogmouth On Prohibition

The tawny frogmouth came to me very late one night
It was very early in the morning and it spoke very quiet
Us tawny frogmouths are spirits of the dead
Who died from overdoses and systemic violence" he said
"I have something important to say and this is my position
Humans will not be free until YOU END PROHIBITION
I'm a tawny frogmouth and I see your frustration
With the punitive justice drug war of incarceration
Thousands of non criminal users each year locked and jailed
But violent crime rates have fallen, the drug war has failed
80 percent of the justice system is wasted each year
Locking up people for flowers and herbs, you are queer
It is obvious to me that prohibition has failed
When you can harm minimise and empty most of the jails
Make access to safe herbs and drugs a right
Save billions of taxpayers dollars overnight
The police could focus on corruption and violent crime
Harm minimisation means there'd be less people dying
Harm minimisation means that you support safe herb users

Educate and rehabilitate the hard poison drug abusers
Less Overdoses and violent crime gangs will fade away
When you grow herbs freely at home, juice cannabis each day
It is obvious to me that you must End Prohibition
Call your politicians today is your mission
And explain all the benefits of ending the war
On women, children, sick, elderly, coloured and poor
I've come to visit you early in the morning
Because you are the one who will sound my warning
We wise tawny frogmouths think you humans are very strange
You seem so conservative and reluctant to embrace change
Mothers are in jail, Nanas in there too
All because of the herbal cannabis they grew
Prohibition is an attack on human rights
It is such an injustice, I have trouble sleeping at night
When prohibition exists people live in fear
Of truth and being caught, imprisoned for a year
Please reconsider your perspective on prohibition of drugs
Free the plants and herbs and undercut the thugs
When you end prohibition there will be a reduction in crime
With harm minimization, there will be less parents crying
When you end prohibition billions of dollars will be saved
Less cops, prisons, lawyers, deaths, more health and happiness every day
I haven't nearly finished, I would love to go to sleep
But I find it very difficult because I often weep
For the victims of the drug war, those overdosed and dead
Brothers, sisters, children's deaths from cop kicks to the head
But now I want to talk about
How women are being imprisoned throughout

The World increasingly putting sisters inside
Victims of a system and the men that deride
The Women that speak up and tell all the truth
About the sex offenders and sexual abuse
A misogynist system of women incarcerated
While Abusive men walk free and women left frustrated
Assaulted by judges, Johns and police
Women made homeless and sleep on the streets
With a back to the wall and one eye half open
For fear of being robbed, raped or groping
She hasn't slept well, she's psychotic, insane
Chemically restrained, injected, sectioned again
"I want voluntary admission to the psych ward," she cries
Injected and pushed back onto the streets to meet KPIs
Back in the street screams and rants
In the back of the police car a hand down her pants
In a cell of the watch house the cycle starts again
Raped by judges and police she questions if she's sane
In a cycle that sees so many lives lost
The Prison Industrial Complex has a high social cost
Do you get it?
It's enough!
The punitive justice system is unjust
Abused in a system and have to prostitute themselves
Intravenous diseases, STDs, Mental Health
I know you agree NOW is the time
For my message to you, people ARE DYING
From prohibition and being in prison
While violent crime falls incarceration has risen
And in 20 years has doubled in Australia

Where the punitive justice system is a failure
The female prison population has doubled
In less than 18 years I'm feeling troubled
From 7 to 14 percent of the prison population
I provide these figures for your information
In 1950 only 4000 people were in detention
Over 40 thousand now. Here is my intention
It's time you reduced incarceration
Restorative justice will end this frustration
And prisons must all be de-privatised
No more making laws to meet KPIs
Most of the prison population is nonviolent
In for prohibition or fraud of money misspent
Nonviolent crimes and illiteracy
90% of the prison population should be free
In the last five years an increase of 30%
When violent crime is falling, your system is bent
It criminalises the socially vulnerable, sick, women, black and poor
There's a much better way for you to restore
The broken and traumatised locked up inside
With caring, assistance, forgiveness applied
To the injustice system that people don't trust
To make it compassionate and truly just
And simplify laws to eliminate state harm
Of forceful imprisonment and police twisting your arm
You can make a system that has love and heart
First ending prohibition would be a wonderful start
And the money saved from excess police and jails
Put to helping minimise abuse because the drug war has failed
To rehabilitate and help those imprisoned inside

So that when they are free they are successful in their lives
The wise tawny frogmouth hooted. The words he spoke were true
"I'm a tawny frogmouth, that is what you need to do"
When you end all prohibition everything will be alright
Maybe then I'll get some sleep at night"

3

Love and Lust in Nimbin

Love and Lust in Nimbin
It could have been apples and appease,
Or sleeping on a doorstep
or smelling of blue cheese
Love and lust in Nimbin
It could be "living in a human zoo"
Or Angry Fascist Bully Boys
Or Rainbow Hippie Spew
Love and Lust in Nimbin
It could have been Aquarius and Peace
Or OD on a Saturday morning
Communes, Cannabis and Trees
Love and Lust in Nimbin
Our eternal dreamtime too
And songs for our corroborees
For our Widjabal ancestors too
Love and Lust in Nimbin
It's what came to my mind
I'm living in the country
I'm eating peaches all the time
Love and Lust in Nimbin

Take a peek inside
You'll love this little town
You'll love it, you'll decide

Ode to the drumming circle in Nimbin

Drumming dancing in the street
Nimbins where the people meet
Drumming all in unity
Party on community
The drumming circle is kind of square
Clarinet and dreadlock hair
Banging on the tambourine
Spontaneous Nimbin party scene
Remember this is Bundjalung
Respect the elders land and sun
Drumming in the Nimbin Way
All the hippies dance and play
Friday night the drums appear
Dancing, singing, straight and queer
Mono, poly, trans or gay
acceptance is the Nimbin way

The Fire's Aftermath

The best coffee in town, no alcohol needed
Picks you up when you are down, hydro, hash, bush seeded
The rainbow cafe has burnt down, the place has been deleted
They burnt it right down to the ground, a rebuild is what's needed
The Lane Way is no more, it's now a concrete path
Mingle Park has a garden now in the fire's aftermath
The best marijuana in town. There's no alcohol needed
Picks you up when you are down, hydro, bush or eaten
The Marijuana Museum has burnt down. The place has been deleted
But Nimbin pulls together now, the locals can't be beaten
The Hemp market has started now, there's chalk art on the path
There's music, dancing in the street in the fire's aftermath

6

This is the sign you are looking for: Gurrimah

A chattering woman says "Chemtrails in the sky"
An uncle, a crow, a friend walking by
A grandma with children. Man and a woman from Rome
A boy selling medicine. Two dogs meet at home
A traveller walking. Tony saying' "Hello"
Medical cannabis heals you know
"I'm sittin' here watchin' the world goin' round"
Uncle Gilbert said to a friend he'd called just now
A bang from the beer truck, poison for poor
Ngalingar Gurrimah brings us together for sure
It means, care and respect and no jealousy
And having no judgement of you or of me
  (Ngalingar Gurrimah is a Bundjalung word meaning We together to care for, respect, have no judgement or jealousy)

7

This is the sign you are looking for and? Part 2 Shane the Cannabis Dealer

Out and about in Nimbin Town
The Bully Boys are walking around
Locking up the herbal healer
Locking up Shane the Cannabis dealer
What can he do, it's so unfair?
The bully boys they just don't care
Persecuting the cannabis dealing
While alcohol does harm not healing
The government they want your money
To tax the sick they think it's funny.
When cannabis is just an herb
Taxes and licenses are absurd
Cannabis must be free
To grow and juice and heal me
I stand here in my defiance
Shouting about the plant freedom alliance
The war on drugs is going down
The bully boys in Nimbin Town

They're searching for the herbal healer
They've locked up Shane the Cannabis dealer
What else can he do? He cannot read
So he supplies the medical cannabis you need
While alcohol harms right across the land
The government's deception's grand
The pharmaceuticals want your money
They poison you and think it's funny
To control the plants it is strange
When plants, animals, humans are free range
Free the herbs for you and me
Medicinal plants must be free
To help with wellness and self reliance
I grow herbs in my defiance
Crime gangs profit from the drug war
The policy men exploit the poor
The drug war's pure discrimination
Punitive justice right across the nation
Corporate, prison, industrial drug war
Targets young men, the black and poor
Making profits by making life hell
Punish your healing so drugs sell
There is a solution called harm minimise
Where people can grow and herbs legalised
It would be a health boost for the cannabis user
Then we could rehab the hard drug abusers
If you legalise drugs you end the black money
Pharmaceutical crime gangs don't think its funny
Because legalising herb means their profits are lower
You could grow your own medicine as a cannabis grower

Drug gangs disappear if we end the drug war
We stop locking up the young men, black and poor
If we end the drug war we help out the healer
And the cops wouldn't lock up Shane the Cannabis dealer

8

Just

Just one
Just one word, one action
Just one man or woman
Just one moment
Just one decision
Ask just one question
Just is everything
Just us
Just standing as one
Just ice
Just ice rings
Just one dealer Just one profiting
Just one life skating on thin ice
Is there any justice or is it just us?
Just us on ice
Just not nice
Just mandatory reporting of ice
No justice
Just your kids they need protection
Just taken away not just ice
Just medicated mummy

No! Just ice.
Just legalise drugs would be nice
Just harm minimise
Just legalise
Is it just ice?
Is it just us?
Is there any justice?
Is it unjust?
Just end prohibition.
Justice is just unjust

9

An Oasis

Nicabate stop smoking aid
Chewed cocaine, sugar lemonade
A can of coke adds life maybe?
Smoking harms your unborn baby
Coffee injected in a vein
Ancient scissors feel no pain
I haven't had a hangover since stopping alcohol
Mushroom down a rabbit hole
MDMA, pingas ecstasy
A giant Shiva Cannabis tree
Oil, hash, cookies and more
It's amazing what you can score
LSD once, twice or thrice
And you should never touch the ice
Bliss balls, hemp balls, chai and more
but friends is the best thing that you can score
in any OASIS
Yeah friends
Friends is the best score that you will ever have

10

Legalise Lettuce

Legalise
Harm minimise
Decriminalise
Legitimise
No more drug war
No more money spent policing
Chasing innocents relaxing
Recreational and healing little herb like lettuce.
Like lettuce?
Lettuce, yes lettuce.
Let us eat a seed of a harmless little weed.
Let us make a tea.
Oil of a flower from a tree.
Let us share it all about,
Cannabis will heal your gout
Let us stop consuming poisons for their TAX.

Legalise
Harm minimise
Decriminalise
Legitimise

No more inmates
No more prisons
No more money social engineering
Chasing innocents relaxing
Victimising home-grown medicine and healing little food.
like lettuce.
Lettuce? yes lettuce.
Let us smoke cannabis
Bongs and pipes of cannabis.
Let us eat our cannabis
Oil of a flower from a tree.
Let us share it all about,
Cannabis may heal your gout
Let us stop consuming poisons for their TAX.

The Yoga Wars

The following poem was written after a Mardi Grass organising meeting in 2018 where Michael Boulderstone mentioned a "class of classes" and "yoga wars"

There was a Clash of classes and Sunny cracked a shit
"I was here before you today," Angel said, "suck it"
"I challenge you to a yoga battle" Sunny said to Angel
This is Warrior one and this one here is table

Sunny with her bleached blond hair and pink leotard
Did cobra and an upward dog and held it very hard
"You ought to salute the sun I was here before you"
Angel didn't flinch and went into Warrior 2

Angel said to Sunny, " Bitch you are a pain"
"You can't afford this leotard I got from Lorna Jane"
Then she didn't salute to the sun and did downward doggy too
She flashed her ass at Sunny and said to her fuck you

Sunny did a cat cow and then a warrior three
She raised herself up tall and did mountain pose and then a tree

JAMES ARTHUR WARREN

Angel took a deep breath and sat in lotus pose
She didn't move and sat there she just thumbed her snotty nose

Sunny took her yoga mat and rolled it very tight
She whacked it into Angels head with all her Yogi might
The Yoga Wars began that day at the rising of the sun
because Angel arrived before Sunny and got the best view of the sun

Burn the Parliament

This piece was written during a Mardi Grass 2018 organizing meeting when Michael Boulderstone suggested that we burn a replica of parliament and everyone cheered like pirates.

Burn the Parliament he said
and the pirates all went argh
I've got a better idea Number 2 said
"Let's do it from afar"
Pirate number 3 she said
"Let's build a fake parliament
We'll put it on a trailer
and cover it in green hemp cement
Pirate number 4
Didn't want to be out done
We'll paint it with marijuana leaves
and leave it in the sun
Pirate number 5
The pirate who was wise
I've got another better idea
Let's make a super big surprise
Let's make that parliament
Open in the middle

and out of it can come Prime Minister
Nero playing the fiddle
Yo ho ho and no more Rum
15 men on a dead man's chest
Yo ho ho and a bottle of rum
Smoked cannabis some more
Pirate number 6 said
this is what we will do
because we have fake parliament
fake politicians too
then we will blow it up
we'll blow parliament Sky High
we'll do it from afar
Just like Guy Fawkes did once try
but Guy Fawkes didn't succeed
he got thrown in a Cell
because he tried to blow up real parliament
he made his own life hell
Then they burnt him on a pyre
that's how we got bonfire night
because that was the very night
that they set poor Guy Fawkes alight
So what we're going to do,
the pirates said we'll do it here
no rum or alcohol or wine
or drinking of the beer
we'll blow up a fake parliament
we will set it all on fire
and then we'll all smoke joints
and everyone will get much higher

burn down the parliament he said
and the pirates all went off their head
We've got a mighty fine idea
Lets smoke cannabis, not drink beer
Yo ho ho and no more rum
Smoke cannabis some more
So the pirates built their fake parliament
And set it very high
it opened in the middle
with Scot fiddling from inside
and then a big boom happened
and the parliament caught fire
And Guy Fawkes wasn't there
Coz it was me who lit the fire
There in the middle of the burning parliament
Of red, yellow, black and brown
Was the government of Australia
Symbolically burnt down
Yo ho ho and no more rum
Let's burn the parliament
Burn the parliament he said
And the Pirates all went off their head
"Burn the parliament"
Yo ho ho there's no more rum
Lets smoke some joints and more
We'll burn the parliament he said
We'll burn it to the floor
There in the middle of the burning parliament
Of red, yellow, black and brown
Was the government of Australia

Symbolically burnt down
Yo ho ho and no more rum
No rum no more
We're gonna smoke cannabis
Overgrow the government some more.

Big Pharma

Who is this big Pharma?
I'll step on his toes.
Who is this big Pharma?
I'll punch him in the nose.

Medical Cannabis Workshop

Written in the Nimbin Bush Theatre during a talk by medical professionals at the Medical Cannabis workshops.

If you were the parent of a child who was sick, would you give cannabis to your son named Dick?

If you were the wife of a man with cancer would you give cannabis as a life enhancer?

If you were a doctor and you knew a cure, pharmaceutical poisons or a herb that's pure?

If a harmless herb can heal many people, why is it registered, licenced, illegal?

Chorus

It's time that the days of prohibition passed

Free up the healing herb and free up the Grass

If a healing herb heals not harms, why does the government twist our arm?

The Earth gives plants for the people to eat, why is cannabis stopped growing in the street?

If the drug war harms people everyday, let's end prohibition today.

If ending prohibition will harm minimise, let's end prohibition without licence disguise.

Chorus

It's time that the days of prohibition passed

Free up the healing herb and free up the Grass

Because cannabis makes your body feel well, locking up users is abuse and hell.

If we end the drug war we help out the people and we could end the big pharmaceutical evil.

If we could grow our own cannabis in our own homes, we could drink it and juice it and smoke a few cones,

Chorus

It's time that the days of prohibition passed

Free up the healing herb and free up the Grass

If cannabis enhances performance and brains, why is prohibition causing us pains?

If cannabis was to be grown and made legal, we'd reduce the poisonous alcohol evil.

If we end all prohibition at the end of the day, there'll be health and less pain and crime gangs will fade away.

If we call all politicians and give them a reason, we could end prohibition of cannabis this growing season.

14

The Notice Board of Dreams

Here in the street where we make dreams.
Not lonely and lost with direction it seems.
Twenty two million to be won Superdraw Saturday
Twenty Three million with a Mega Jackpot play
Woofers are wanted to clean up my land
Pulling lantana to give me a hand
Tuntable bush dance happening next week
Waters are running down in the creek
Caravan for sale if you want a home
Barry's mowing service, brush cutting lawns mown
Foraging and survival skills taught at reWild,
Learn a skill set for an outdoor wild child
Awakening woman free workshop one day
Tristan the tradie odd jobs any day
Forest Temple Sharehouse practice meditation
Do you know your true purpose? And a missing alsation
Hula Hoop Dance for beginners fit, fun, fantastic
Nimbin Youth film festival make a film like Jurassic
Two sister milking goats are up for sale
Betwixt and Between Hanging Rock Hall Wadeville
Kinesiology massage flower essences too

POETRY TO END PROHIBITION

Federal Park Party stalls and artisan food
Nexus secret history of Australia conference at Mullumbimby
Acupuncture Earth Dragon Chinese Therapy
I'd like to have a house swap for a couple of weeks
I've a two bedroom in Byron at Sunrise Beach
Please don't use 1080 baits on your land
Four Canadian backpackers willing to lend a hand
Let's get physical comedy at the Town Hall
Hillary's cleaning service attention to all
At the Bush Theatre the fun never ends
Medical Cannabis Workshop this weekend
Art in the park weather permitting Friday
Queer Karaoke You don't have to be gay
Diana Anaid leaving town soon
Birth and beyond community room
Nimbin Family playgroup Tuesday and Friday
Come celebrate the 20th annual Big Scrub Rainforest Day
Nia will make you feel alive
Hatha Vinyasa yoga starts at 5
Osteopathy reiki at the inner sanctum
Dreadlocks fixed naturally, I'll reskin your drum
Cleaner available please call Joanne
Leaving Australia selling my Hiace Van
Island Vibe Festival 20 18
Josepe Signing Nimbin Hills Magazine
Earth Building Workshop, build your home on your land
Online herbalist to give you a hand
Mugwort is wanted enquire within
Weave and Mend festival learn to weave and to spin
Penelope Pranna morning sun salutations

Untangle with swift affordable custom meditation
Coming up soon Blue Moon Cabaret
Blue Cat Swing Gollan Hotel Saturday
Chihuaha Shitsu microchipped vaccination
Come join our family's memorial celebration
Here in the street of where we make dreams
Entrepreneurs with new direction it seems

16

Stoned or High?

Today the best insult someone could come up with was "stoner". This is incorrect as I am a fully recovered alcoholic. The etymology of the word stoned was first recorded in use in 1945 in reference to being intoxicated with alcohol. Like being knocked down with a stone, stoned or stone cold drunk. The word "stone" referring to a small rock has Germanic and Dutch origins in the English language. Jack Kerouac used the word in 1951 in On The Road.

Through the mid 60s the word was used for a "stuporous person" It was only in the 1980s that the word stoned and stoner was used for people generally under the influence of consciousness and physical altering or enhancing substances like Heroin or Cannabis. Now since I have never experienced "stupor" from Cannabis use alone as I have from alcohol use or mixing substances, I much prefer to use the term *high as it refers to the performance enhancing and positive emotional state induced by THC, CBD, as well as the healing properties of eating, smoking and Cannabis rubbing oils.

Let's make sure we correctly use the word stoned for people who are stupefied by poisons and not as an insult to my intelligence.

JAMES ARTHUR WARREN

Ice

This one is dedicated to Nicolette Papadopoulos of The Nimbin Oasis who asked me to write something to reclaim the word "ice" as the meaning for our sacred water and the source of all life, in its frozen state.

There is this stuff that's pure and crystalline.
Frozen water is called ice.
Cools you on a hot day and makes you feel nice.
Ice is a frozen snowflake, hail and an igloo.
But methamphetamine should be called brain frying glue.
I was walking down the street with a bag of party ice.
He joked, "get out of town we don't want you dealing ice"
It made me feel sad that our water clean and pure
Is now the slang for Crystal Meth a poison that's for sure.
Because water gives you energy and cleans you that's for sure
But crystal meth fries your brain and is so impure.
I went along my way and added water to my ice
Drank it up and cooled down I was feeling nice
A thirsty stranger came along with a thirsty daughter.
I poured them both a glass of ice with cold cold water.
After just one sip both their eyes lit up
We are feeling better with ice water in our cup.
I am feeling great and no longer feeling down
My daughter drank your icy water and no longer wears a frown.
I hear the cops in New South Wales are corrupt and dealing meth
They have ulterior motives to addict the youth to death
Cannabis will soon be legal and cops are worried about KPIS so dealing meth
Will keep them in employment and prisons full that's why they are dealing death.

We can end the prohibition and minimise the harm
Then the coppers will not need to search and twist your arm
If we end drug prohibition right across the nation
We'd get rid of corrupt coppers and 80% of the prison population.
Make access to safe drugs a right and make it safe and clean
As water falling from the sky and snowflakes so pristine
Let's all stop the drug war and the coppers dealing death
And claim the word "ice " once more for frozen water and not crystal meth

17

They locked up my nana

Written for Tanya McDonald who was arrested in Nimbin for selling Choc Chip Cannabis Cookies.

Grandma what did you do?
Grandma. Where have they taken you?
Grandma helping people healing
Grandma was cannabis choc chip cookie dealing
They locked up my grandma and took her away
Allegedly selling home baked cookies in Nimbin today
selling her cookies to help others healing
The charge 1.8 kilograms of cannabis dealing
Cookies with choc chips sugar and flour
Cannabis butter slow cooked for 6 hours
Her cookies were famous in every land
New York, Paris and the Netherlands
Selling healing cookies they took her away
I saw the police arrest my grandma today
They banished my grandma from our community
For selling healing cookies with impunity
They said to my grandma get out of town
We don't want you healing people around
they locked up my grandma and took her away

Alleged she was selling choc chip cookies they say.
End the drug war on people who want to self heal
Leave alone the grandmas who choc chip cookie deal.
It's time that we adopt harm minimization
End prohibition of drugs change this situation
The benefits to society would be heaven sent
We could empty the prisons by 80%
They locked up my grandma, carted her away
Punitive justice needs to end today
Ending prohibition improves social conditions
And not FEAR THE TRUTH of government prohibition
It's time that we got rid of outdated laws
Stopped locking up grandmas fathers, black and poor
Because they locked up my grandma today
For selling choc chips cookies they say.

Stinky Bong Bill

Stinky Bong Bill had a smelly bong
he hadn't changed his bong water for ten years long
Stinky Bong Bill's water never made him ill
He'd gargle and spit back that vile swill
Stinky Bong Bill's water never made him sick
Even though it was black, muddy, putrid and thick
Smelling like bitumen, sewage, vomit and piss
It stopped others from smoking Bill's cannabis
No one else wanted one of Stinky Bong Bills cones
His bong stunk out all his whole home
Except Stinky Bong Bill's friend who's name was Fred
Who said to Bill "Give me a smoke of your head
From your stinky bong with the putrid black water
"Can I have a cone? I think you ought to"
Give me a cone" said Stinky Bong Bill's friend Fred
So he packed a cone with one of his biggest heads
He sucked down the cone through Stinky Bong Bill's Bong
And he got very sick and it didn't take very long
Because Fred wasn't ready for Bill's stinky Bong
It made him so sick, he vomited all night long
With, diarrhea, staph, legionnaires and dysentery

He spent the whole night driving the lavatory
Pneumonia, whooping cough and bong water on the lung
Fred nearly died at only 20 years young
Stinky Bong Bill got sick that night and started to spew
Went to hospital in an ambulance and Fred went too
Bill now cleans his bong daily with metho and rice
With fresh rain water his smoke now smells nice
Bill didn't lose out and now smokes more Cannabis
His friends now have a chance they wouldn't want to miss
The chance to smoke from one of Bill's collection of bongs
From bong designers worldwide there's one 3 meters long
With twenty three chambers all pristine clean
Made from Baccarat Crystal as smooth as a dream
Bill has bongs from every nation and land
Internationally recognised bong collection as grand
Some bongs are silver and some are gold
One bong is over three thousand years old
Bill cleans his bongs daily and he's not so silly
And is known worldwide as "Long Bong Clean Willy"

19

Write your own prohibition poetry on this page.

Crack hole

A shit hole a turd hole and not a nice place.
People go there just to get off their face

Crack heads and ice heads the violent and poor
Little wonder people avoid going there any more

In need of a paint job, a spruce and a clean
And ambient music you know what I mean
Because people now only go to get high
Crack ice and heroin if you're desperate to try
The impure cut drugs caused by prohibition
Instead of harms minimised if we changed the condition

ODed or psychosis and haven't slept for days
Fear of the truth of his drug taking ways
And being locked in prison for self medicating
No chance of rehab from the drugs that he's taking

Crystal Meth made in a basement he's wired
Hasn't slept for three days but he's not tired

Adrenaline rush and he's running again
Speaking to himself and going insane
    Too many rushes in uncontrolled doses
Being carted away and in a psychosis
Certified by a shrink as partially insane
Pharmaceutical poison forcefully injected in his brain
Walking dribbling like a zombie with tears in his eyes
Meeting cops and psychologists KPIs
Prohibition causes many social pains
Harms aren't minimised, there's many fried brains
    Ending all prohibition would change the situation
    We could harm minimise right across the nation
    And empty the prisons by eighty percent
    And save billions of dollars if prohibition went
    Then people could grow Cannabis at home
    Eat it, juice and cook it and feel good all alone
    From a flower of a tree that you grow for free
    Not pharmaceutical poisons, free the cannabis tree
    No OD from opiates choked on vomit alone
    They found him on the floor dead in his own home
    And the whole place stank from the shit of the mouse
    A shit hole, a turd hole the junkie's crack house

Prohibition

For decades prohibition has caused drug use to rise
    So to fill up the prisons that have been privatised
    Prohibition of drugs funds dealers in crime
    Because of these outdated laws there are people dying
    From cut, impure, unsafe drugs they are taking

He OD'd on Oxycontin and was never waking
As we pumped and we blew trying to keep him alive
I met his mum, dad, brother, sister after he died
Jailing drug users is abuse and unjust
Self medicating users fear the truth and don't trust
Fear of the truth and being locked in a prison
Means reluctance to seek help and no harm minimism
Mums, dads, the young, poor and black locked away
Prohibition damages the socially vulnerable everyday
People aren't protected with drug prohibition
Drug related crime soars and so does drug addiction
There is a solution where drug use is legalised
A new policy adopted to harm minimise
Then we nurture, support and care for drug users
And stop the punitive justice and prison abusers
Caused by the systemic injustice and abuse by the state
There's seventy seven thousand users they incarcerate
And take them from families and support systems too
We are poor because dad's locked in jail, it's true
And the children are taken away by the court
From a Family Services mandatory report
Of mummy an occasional smoker of weed
Prohibition harms in many ways indeed

21

Pizzaster

The Giant Orgy of gluttony and lust begins
and holly day pride all partakes in the sins
Of the fertility Goddess Ishtar now Easter,
let's go to Byron Bay Blues fest and Pizza,
Camping and touring with bikes on the rear
to make the most of the last 4 public holidays of the year
I got seven days off using two sickies
between Easter and ANZAC day and being tricky
Beer battered fish and chips, "Dad I want maccas"
Stop your fucking whining it's driving me crackers
There's no fucking McDonalds here in Byron Bay,
You"ll get you fucking Pizza at the end of the day
Byron Bay Easter time there's always rain
"Let's go for a drive and stop being a pain"
Let's visit Nimbin I heard it is pretty
A small colourful town and not like the city
"Hey Buddy you want to buy cookies or weed?"
"I've mushrooms as well whatever you need"
"I got us some brownies for when the kids go to bed
"Cannabis brownies we'll get off our head"
Kids dragged about shops with light flowing frocks

and rainbow chimes ringing, handicraft shops
Market's of farm produce, craft and imports
Now footy season's full swing there's so many sports
games that I have to view,
let go back to the hotel room I've got something to do
Heads down in iPads and glows of smartphones
On family holidays but isolated alone
"I'm hungry" "Wait till dinner, I promised you pizza"
The line up was 30 minutes because it was Easter
Then finally the pizza after a two hour wait
and the pasta arrived after that one hour late
Lola whined constantly I wanted a toy
I've the whole happy meal set except the boy toy
with her bottom lip hanging and wearing a frown
whining and whinging she wore me down
I was bubbling furious and just about to crack
but Lola my little girl kicked my ball sack
under the table and I gave a loud yell
that silenced the whole restaurant and the line up as well
As I hit the roof, lost my temper, when crackers
The day that my little girl kicked me in the knackers
Just as the police walked in for a pizza
I was arrested for disrupting the peace there that Easter
And Cannabis cookies on our holiday in Byron Bay
fingerprinted, bailed and in court on Tuesday.
And that is my story of the Pizza Disaster of Easter
the Pizzaster, in Byron at Fat Piggies Pizza

22

The voices of the dead

I went to visit the dead today
At the cemetery and listen to what they had to say
"We are the dead and the victims of laws
And injustice the ones that died from your wars
People keep dying please change this condition
Of your injustice system called drug prohibition
There were mothers and fathers and young people we grieve
He died from FLACA at 23, one New Years Eve
Writhing and screaming he was overheating
Boom Boom Boom of the Doof then his heart just stopped beating
A whole family but the baby died in a smash
Of an alcoholic driver who had a car crash
The beaten and murdered children and wives
When pissed dad arrived home who feared for their lives
Let's not forget those who died from cancer
Who couldn't access cannabis as a life enhancer
Prohibition of drugs is social abuse
Locking up people for recreational use
Did you hear about how young Jake M died?
ODed from the drugs his mother supplied
Prohibition of drugs is an outdated law

POETRY TO END PROHIBITION

That criminalises the socially vulnerable, sick, black and poor
Police become dealers and deal drugs
To justify their jobs and do deals with thugs
Selling black market heroine, cocaine and ice
To keep prisons full and meet KPIs
Racially profiling the coloured and poor
Died in the lock up, crushed behind a cell door
As I sit here I am looking down at the ground
Where I performed CPR on a young man who drowned
Choked on his vomit we tried but he died
I met his mum dad and siblings and we all cried
Today I went to honour the dead
At Nimbin Cemetery and this is what I said
Dead spirits I'd love it if you would help me
Harm Minimise, End Prohibition and make Cannabis Free
If I was a teacher I would give you a fail
For your punitive justice system and the way that you jail
The sick, poor and black recreational users
When it is clear to all that the system abuses
Drug prohibition doesn't stop demand for drugs
Just puts it in the hands of criminals and thugs
The cost of prohibition is millions each year
To imprison the harmless and put people in fear
Harm minimisation is good for your health
Sharing and caring and rehabilitate yourself
I went to the cemetery and listened to the dead
End All Prohibition" their spirits all said

Healing Herb Haiku

Handcuffs hurting tight
Twisted arm and dragged away
Harmless healing herb

Prohibition is corrosive

In response to an article in the Australian where some top cop.said,
"Drugs are corrosive and cause social deconstruction"
I continued,
"When the police become dealers and participate in corruption
Bahahahahah
Because Prohibition is destructive and causes more pain
Jailing self medicating medicine users is absurd and strange
Sydney has a very high use of coke
Solicitors and mummy's, prohibition is a joke
So locking up users in prison is abuse
To end prohibition there is no excuse
Social disruption daddy's locked away
So we don't have food on the table today
Deconstruction of family mummy is jailed
It is easily seen prohibition has failed
You don't reduce demand and supply is a crime
One hundred thousand dollars a year for one person's time
To be incarcerated, criminalised, a victim of the State's
Punitive punishment system which incarcerates
The poor, black and coloured, the mums and dads
Which corrupts the family and deconstructs that.

We could harm minimise like the Portuguese
End the drug war and social disease
We'd empty the prisons if we legalize
And ending prohibition will save millions of lives
Empty most prisons when we release
The victims and we will need many less police
Saving billions of dollars a year and reduce crime
Rehabilitation of abusers instead of doing time
And grow cannabis, grow brain cells and get rid of pains
Stop alcohol poisoning and destroying brains.
Prohibition is corrosive and causes social deconstruction
It encourages criminals and police corruption

End Prohibition for my Grandma

Grandma is smoking cannabis again,
She's laughing, giggling and smoking with her friend
Grandma likes only the best weed
Bakes it and vapes it and also makes teas
She used to have cancer but now she is good
It grows in her vegetable garden and is a staple food
Grandma is high and she's smoking medicinal weed
She gives it to her friends and they love her indeed
Grandma smokes bongs, joints and big pipes
She is always happy and never gripes
Now grandma is happy and grandma alive
I'm also happy cannabis made my grandma survive

Weeds

What is a weed but an unwanted plant?
Cannabis is not a weed, my end prohibition rant
Flowers are medicine and seeds are a food
Fibre, food medicine, cannabis is good
And Cannabis should be free to grow in our homes
Like lettuce, please free us to eat, juice and grow
The most useful plant that must grow for free
Let us end prohibition and free the Cannabis tree
A weed could be silverleaf goat fed or sorrel
Cobblers Peg flour, medicinal camphor Laurel
In the Everglades Melaleuca and America Eucalyptus
But thanks for all the medicines the wild weeds give us
Bananas are giant herbs and grow like weed
But our DNA has traits of bananas indeed
Let weeds be our medicine and weeds be our food
To view weeds as unwanted is limiting, judgemental and crude.
I've got a friend and his name is Dave Tree
He comes from far away and he's a weed like me
But weeds are quite useful and good medicine
To eliminate all weeds would be a big sin

Shakespeare Inhaled

Dost thou inhale
The silver sweet smoke of medicinal weed?
Shakespeare inhaled but not strange compounds dost he need.
To smoke or to not but I questioneth what
Art thou inhaling the weed smoke or art thou not?
Huble and bubble thee chalice bong bubble
Cauldrons of butter and cannabis bubble
Not a strange compound.
It is to be
Writing midsummer night sonnets
Thou dost smoketh the weed

Tawny Frogmouth's Pain- The Sixth Visit

Last night I went for a drive to collect some eucalyptus seeds so that I can grow some seedlings to plant trees for koala corridors. It was just on dusk and the tawny frogmouth was sitting peacefully on the driveway. I got out of my ute and approached him. Then he majestically flew off into the night. This is the message that he ;eft with me last night.

The Tawny Frogmouth came again last night and said,

"I hate to be a pain, but prohibition is is causing harm to livers and damage to the brain"

There are so many people who want to medicate themself,

but they can't get real medicine so end up damaging their health"

Cannabis is prohibited but cures cancer and also pain

Magic mushrooms cure depression, reset and reactivate your brain

DMT is made by your lungs, in your pineal gland in roots and bark of trees for free

It is one of the most endogenously produced and healing substances denied from you and me

Alcohol is a poison and damages your liver and brain

But marketed and freely sold, prohibition is insane"

The Tawny Frogmouth said, "take a long hard look at yourself

Why prohibit medicines but sell what is bad for your health?
We tawny frogmouth owls wonder if you humans are sane?
Why do you drink alcohol which damages your kidneys and your brain
You would be better off without alcohol," the tawny frogmouth said
But magic mushrooms, cannabis, harmaline and DMT grow new brain cells in your head
"I am a psychedelic tawny frogmouth, I just love and wish you well
And that you recover from your alcoholism that makes you unwell and your life hell. "
Please, I love you, please, I love you, I'll ask you once again
Please care and nurture your own health, I am crying here in pain"
The Tawny frogmouth came last night and this is what he said
"Please stop drinking alcohol, " I heard him in my head.

Dedicated to Daniel the Lion

1/8/2017
I arrived in Nimbin in early May 2017 for Mardi Grass and met another newcomer to Nimbin by the name of Daniel Walmsley. Daniel was a kind young man in his mid twenties and talented artist who had just received an arts grant. He was excited to be able to do what he loved and be paid for it. Unfortunately for Daniel he overdosed and choked in his vomit early one Saturday morning. I happened to be going for an early morning walk when I came across a nurse trying to resuscitate Daniel and gave assistance

The following poem is dedicated to the memory of Daniel and all the victims of the "War on drugs" which is really a war on people who were not able to get safe doses when they were self medicating because of the punitive justice system which puts "users" in to "fear of truth", hiding their addictions and unable to get assistance in recovery.

Daniel Walmsley

It started on a cold Friday
The drumming circle, dance and play
All the families gathered around
Barefoot on the cold hard ground
Drummers drumming having fun
Stomping feet down goes the sun
Fires burning in the parks
Shooting stars and burning sparks
Rhythmic hands all beat it out
The drumming circle dance about
Nimbin on a Friday night
Drum and dance by fire light
They bring their drums out to the street
Where dancing feet move to the beat
Dreadlocks smokes it clean and green
He beats his blue drum with the team
Down by the fire at the Oasis
There's lots of friends and friendly faces
Try this hit, it won't hurt you
He overdoses and starts to spew
Starts the walk to hospital

"I'm OhDee-ing" He starts to call
Falls down to the cold hard ground
In his vomit starts to drown
Nurse and passers by all thump
On his heart they start to pump
"Call an ambulance" they cry
"Daniel, Daniel, please don't die
CPR the people start
Giving breath and pumping heart
Police and ambulance arrived
For forty five minutes we all tried
Sun comes up cold Saturday
Daniel's soul flies away
Leaving behind broken hearts
Drawing and paintings of Daniel's arts
Overdosed on cold concrete
Laying dead with cold bare feet
End prohibition right now, today
Harm minimisation saves lives we say
Laying on the cold hard ground
His heart stopped and just shut down
His life might be a memory
End prohibition for safety

After word

My belief is that the day where all prohibition of drugs is near and harm minimisation will become normal.

It is only by standing in our power and educating those that do not understand the consequences and social damage done by prohibition that we can bring about the change required.

When prohibition ends we shall then be able to legally use safe performance enhancing natural medicines like cannabis, magic mushrooms and DMT in "Clubs with no beer", and hopefully then people will stop poisoning themselves with alcohol. As I write this I am feeling the pain of all those affected by prohibition and tears are streaming from my eyes.

Please assist me in the collective dream to end prohibition forever.

Maybe then I'll get some sleep at night.

The Seventh Visit of the Tawny Frogmouth

The tawny frogmouth came last night and this is what he had to say
"Thundercloud it's time to get your words published and underway
The tawny frogmouth came and this is exactly what he said
"Publish your Prohibition book before more people are dead
The tawny frogmouth came with important news
Thundercloud publish your book so that it gets many views
The tawny frogmouth came last night and told me what ot do
Publish "Poetry to End Prohibition in time for 420 2020 That's what you've got to do
Here I'm sitting now with this message from my friend
I am Thundercloud Repairian and this is the End
The Seventh time the tawny frog came to me
He said, "Thundercloud publish your end prohibition poetry."
12/3/2020

33

The End of Prohibition

On this day the thirteenth of March, in the year two thousand and twenty, I, James Arthur Warren do declare that for the collective risk and harm reduction and nurturance of life, that it is our collective common right to consume any naturally growing plant and fungi, including but not limited to fruit, nuts, leaves, bark, mycelium, fungi or vegetable provided that it enhances and not damages the performance and wellness of the sacred human vessel.

I declare that harm minimisation is the normal policy of care and this is

the end of drug prohibition and the end of the drug war.
This is the end of drug prohibition in New South Wales.
This is the end of drug prohibition in Australia.
This is the end of drug prohibition on Earth.

This is the beginning of harm minimisation.

www.ingramcontent.com/pod-product-compliance
Lightning Source LLC
Chambersburg PA
CBHW070729020526
44107CB00077B/2343